S

by Iain Gray

Lang**Syne**
PUBLISHING
WRITING *to* REMEMBER

LangSyne

PUBLISHING

WRITING *to* REMEMBER

79 Main Street, Newtongrange,
Midlothian EH22 4NA
Tel: 0131 344 0414   Fax: 0845 075 6085
E-mail: info@lang-syne.co.uk
www.langsyneshop.co.uk

Design by Dorothy Meikle
Printed by Ricoh Print Scotland
© Lang Syne Publishers Ltd 2012

ISBN 978-1-85217-200-8

Shaw

HIGHLAND SHAWS

SEPT NAMES INCLUDE:
Ayson, Easson, Macay, Machay,
Scheach, Shay, Seith

MOTTO: By Fidelity and Fortitude.

CREST: A hand grasping a dagger.

LOWLAND SHAWS

MOTTO: I mean well.

CREST: A savage wielding a cudgel.

"The spirit of the clan means much to thousands of people"

Chapter one:

The origins of the clan system

by Rennie McOwan

The original Scottish clans of the Highlands and the great families of the Lowlands and Borders were gatherings of families, relatives, allies and neighbours for mutual protection against rivals or invaders.

Scotland experienced invasion from the Vikings, the Romans and English armies from the south. The Norman invasion of what is now England also had an influence on land-holding in Scotland. Some of these invaders stayed on and in time became 'Scottish'.

The word clan derives from the Gaelic language term 'clann', meaning children, and it was first used many centuries ago as communities were formed around tribal lands in glens and mountain fastnesses.

The format of clans changed over the centuries, but at its best the chief and his family held the land on behalf of all, like trustees, and the ordinary clansmen and women believed they had a blood relationship with the founder of their clan.

There were two way duties and obligations. An inadequate chief could be deposed and replaced by someone of greater ability.

Clan people had an immense pride in race. Their relationship with the chief was like adult children to a father and they had a real dignity.

The concept of clanship is very old and a more feudal notion of authority gradually crept in.

Pictland, for instance, was divided into seven principalities ruled by feudal leaders who were the strongest and most charismatic leaders of their particular groups.

By the sixth century the 'British' kingdoms of Strathclyde, Lothian and Celtic Dalriada (Argyll) had emerged and Scotland, as one nation, began to take shape in the time of King Kenneth MacAlpin.

Some chiefs claimed descent from

ancient kings which may not have been accurate in every case.

By the twelfth and thirteenth centuries the clans and families were more strongly brought under the central control of Scottish monarchs.

Lands were awarded and administered more and more under royal favour, yet the power of the area clan chiefs was still very great.

The long wars to ensure Scotland's independence against the expansionist ideas of English monarchs extended the influence of some clans and reduced the lands of others.

Those who supported Scotland's greatest king, Robert the Bruce, were awarded the territories of the families who had opposed his claim to the Scottish throne.

In the Scottish Borders country – the notorious Debatable Lands – the great families built up a ferocious reputation for providing warlike men accustomed to raiding into England and occasionally fighting one another.

Chiefs had the power to dispense justice

and to confiscate lands and clan warfare produced a society where martial virtues – courage, hardiness, tenacity – were greatly admired.

Gradually the relationship between the clans and the Crown became strained as Scottish monarchs became more orientated to life in the Lowlands and, on occasion, towards England.

The Highland clans spoke a different language, Gaelic, whereas the language of Lowland Scotland and the court was Scots and in more modern times, English.

Highlanders dressed differently, had different customs, and their wild mountain land sometimes seemed almost foreign to people living in the Lowlands.

It must be emphasised that Gaelic culture was very rich and story-telling, poetry, piping, the clarsach (harp) and other music all flourished and were greatly respected.

Highland culture was different from other parts of Scotland but it was not inferior or less sophisticated.

Central Government, whether in London

Clan warfare produced a society where courage and tenacity were greatly admired

or Edinburgh, sometimes saw the Gaelic clans as a challenge to their authority and some sent expeditions into the Highlands and west to crush the power of the Lords of the Isles.

Nevertheless, when the eighteenth century Jacobite Risings came along the cause of the Stuarts was mainly supported by Highland clans.

The word Jacobite comes from the Latin for James – Jacobus. The Jacobites wanted to restore the exiled Stuarts to the throne of Britain.

The monarchies of Scotland and England became one in 1603 when King James VI of Scotland (1st of England) gained the English throne after Queen Elizabeth died.

The Union of Parliaments of Scotland and England, the Treaty of Union, took place in 1707.

Some Highland clans, of course, and Lowland families opposed the Jacobites and supported the incoming Hanoverians.

After the Jacobite cause finally went down at Culloden in 1746 a kind of ethnic cleansing took place. The power of the chiefs was curtailed. Tartan and the pipes were banned in law.

Many emigrated, some because they wanted to, some because they were evicted by force. In addition, many Highlanders left for the cities of the south to seek work.

Many of the clan lands became home to sheep and deer shooting estates.

But the warlike traditions of the clans and the great Lowland and Border families lived on, with their descendants fighting bravely for freedom in two world wars.

Remember the men from whence you came, says the Gaelic proverb, and to that could be added the role of many heroic women.

The spirit of the clan, of having roots, whether Highland or Lowland, means much to thousands of people.

Chapter two:

Highlanders and Lowlanders

Shaw is a unique surname in Scotland in that it has at least two quite separate and unrelated origins and two distinct families, or kindred, have proudly borne the name throughout Scotland's long and colourful story.

These unrelated families of Shaw have their origins in the lush pasturelands of the Lowlands and the stark beauty of the mist enshrouded mountains of the distant Highlands, and Shaws from both these widely separated geographical areas came to play significant roles in their nation's often bloody history.

In the Highlands, the derivation of Shaw is from the Gaelic 'sithech', meaning a wolf, although another possible derivation is from the Gaelic 'Na 'Si'ach', meaning 'Son of the Tempest', or 'Son of the Snow.' The Old

Celtic version of the name is 'scheagh', or 'sheagh'.

Whatever the original derivation of the name, it is interesting to note that for many centuries 'Shaw' was a forename, and this explains why in the Highlands the Shaws were not known as Clan Shaw, but 'the Shaw' or, in Gaelic, 'Na Siach' or 'Mhic Sheaghid'.

Today, however, Clan Shaw is officially recognised as a Highland clan, and has its own proud motto of 'By fidelity and fortitude', and crest of a hand grasping a dagger.

The Lowland 'Shaw', or 'Schawe', stems from the Old English 'scaga', or 'sceaga', meaning a small area of woodland, and these Lowland Shaws became particularly prominent in Renfrewshire, Lanarkshire, and the Stirling area, with significant numbers also in Greenock, Ayrshire, and Kirkcudbrightshire and the main line of the Lowland Shaws are the Schaws of Sauchie, near Stirling, whose motto is 'I mean well' and whose crest, not particularly in keeping with this sentiment, is a savage wielding a cudgel!

The genealogy of the Highland Shaws is extremely complex, stretching back to the time of an ancient Celtic institution known as the Seven Earls of Scotland.

Originally known as mormaers ('great stewards') or thanes, these earls ruled the seven original Pictish sub-kingdoms in the northeast of Scotland of Atholl, Angus, Mar, Moray, Caithness, Strathearn, and Fife.

Descended from the seven sons of Cruithne, an early Pictish king, they acted as provincial kings and even after the kingdom we now know as Scotland was united under Kenneth MacAlpin in 843 AD, they wielded great power in the selection of a new king on the death of the old.

The earls of Fife, for example, from time immemorial, had the right to perform the sacred ceremony of enthronement of a Scottish king, and it was a Shaw MacDuff, a younger son of a Thane of Fife, who was made keeper of the royal castle of Inverness during the reign from 1153-65 of Malcolm IV.

It is this Shaw MacDuff who is said to be the progenitor, or founder, of what became the distinct clan of Shaw.

Shaw MacDuff's heirs were known as the 'Mhic an Toiseach' ('the sons of the thane', or 'the sons of the chief'), and this Mhic an Toiseach became better known as 'Mackintosh.'

This is why Clan Shaw today, although a clan in its own right, is recognised as a sept, or branch, of Clan Mackintosh.

Through Clan Mackintosh, the Shaws in turn also became members of the mighty confederation of clans known as Clan Chattan, which until as late as the eighteenth century was the main power in the Badenoch region of the Spey Valley.

With its motto of 'Touch not the cat without a glove', and crest of a rampant wildcat (the same as Clan Mackintosh), Clan Chattan also included MacPhersons, Farquharsons, MacThom-ases, McBains, Macleans, McGillivrays and Davidsons in its ranks.

Clan Chattan sided with the cause of

Scotland's independence under the great warrior king Robert the Bruce, and their motley but battle-hardened band of clansmen fought with distinction to help to achieve Bruce's victory over the cream of English chivalry at the battle of Bannockburn, in 1314.

It was Shaw Macghillechrist Mhic Iain, more commonly known as 'Sgorfhiaclach' or 'Bucktooth', who was responsible for consolidating the power of what would become the distinct clan of Highland Shaws, through his prowess as a warrior.

As captain of Clan Chattan, he took part in an infamous raid into the shire of Angus in 1391 that ended in a fierce battle at Glen Brierachan.

Sir Walter Ogilvie of Auchterhouse, Sheriff of Angus, had called out a force of local magnates and lairds to defend the shire from the ravages of Duncan Stewart, a son of Alexander, Earl of Buchan, better known as the Wolf of Badenoch.

Shaw Bucktooth and his Chattan kinsfolk, ever eager for easy pickings, had joined with Stewart, and took part in the slaughter of Sir Walter and his puny force.

Five years later, in 1396, Shaw Bucktooth led the Clan Chattan contingent in the famous Battle of the Clans that took place on a large, flat meadow on the outskirts of Perth known as the North Inch.

A bitter feud had dragged out for some time between Clan Chattan and Clan Kay, a bloody vendetta that had not only visited mayhem on the clans themselves, but also periodically devastated the lives of their more peaceful neighbours.

In a desperate bid to resolve the matter, the monarch, Robert III, arranged for a gladiatorial combat between the two warring factions, watched by not only the king himself but a glittering array of courtiers and even the Dauphin of France.

Sixty champions were chosen from each side, with Shaw Bucktooth commanding the Chattan clansmen.

Armed with a deadly arsenal of swords,

dirks, axes, and allowed to shoot off one volley of crossbow bolts, the 120 warriors battled it out until only eleven Chattans, including Shaw, were left standing on the blood-soaked field of combat.

The sole Kay survivor took to his heels and swam for safety across the River Tay.

Shaw Bucktooth's kin had lived for centuries in Rothiemurchus, but a grateful Mackintosh chief, the head of Clan Chattan, gifted him with possession of these lands 'for all the valour he showed that day against his enemies.'

These lands were sold to the Grants in the sixteenth century, but Adam (or Ay), a grandson of Shaw Bucktooth had acquired lands at Tordarroch, in Strathnairn, in 1468. This family became known as Clan Aedh, or Ay ('the children of Shaw'), and their lands are still held.

The First Marquis of Montrose

*James Graham, the fifth Earl and first
Marquis of Montrose*

In 1970, the Lord Lyon King of Arms of Scotland recognised a Shaw of Tordarroch as 21st chief of Clan Shaw, after a vacancy of 200 years. This confirmed Clan Shaw as 'a line of unbroken continuity from the ancient earls of Fife.'

Septs of Clan Shaw include Ayson, Aison, Easson, MacAy, MacHay, Scaith, Scheach, Schiach, Shaith, Shay, Sheath, and Seith. There are also two Clan Shaw tartans, Shaw of Tordarroch and the green Shaw.

The green Shaw is derived from the regimental tartan of the famous Black Watch, and commemorates a Fearchar Shaw who, along with two of his fellows, was executed at Tower Hill, London, in 1743 for refusing to serve overseas in Britain's foreign wars.

The regiment had mutinied after the government broke its pledge that it would not have to serve overseas, and Fearchar Shaw and his companions were selected as 'examples' to crush further mutiny.

Chapter three:

For the Stuart cause

The Shaws were ardent in their devotion to the Royal House of Stuart throughout all of its tragic misfortunes, and the Shaws of Tordarroch raised a force to join Clan Chattan in its support of the Royalist James Graham, 1st Marquis of Montrose, during his great campaigns from 1644 to 1645 in support of Charles I.

This period became known as the Year of Miracles because of Montrose's brilliant military successes, including victory over the Presbyterian forces of the Earl of Argyll at Inverlochy in February of 1645.

What made this victory all the more remarkable was that his hardy band of clansmen, including Shaws under the Clan Chattan banner, had arrived at Inverlochy after a tortuous 36-hour march south through deep snow from the area of present day Fort Augustus.

Clan Chattan also shared in Montrose's victory at Kilsyth in August of 1645, but also in his defeat at Philiphaugh, near Selkirk, less than a month later.

The Shaws also paid dearly for their support of the Stuart cause in the Jacobite Risings of 1715 and 1745. Jacobite unrest had risen following the Hanoverian succession to the throne under George, Elector of Hanover, in 1714, and in September of the following year the Earl of Mar raised the Royal Standard of the Stuarts at Braemar.

It was at Farr, near Tordarroch, that only a few days later William Mackintosh of Borlum called out Clan Chattan to fight for the cause, and Robert Shaw of Tordarroch and his brother, Angus, led what was described as a highly disciplined and well-equipped contingent of Shaws.

But, plagued by bad leadership and squabbles over what military strategy to adopt, the Jacobite campaign was doomed almost from the start.

The cause was effectively lost following the battle of Sheriffmuir in November, when Mar lost the initiative against the Hanoverian forces led by John Campbell, 2nd Duke of Argyll, by withdrawing to Perth.

Mackintosh of Borlum had meanwhile displayed military genius by managing to cross the Firth of Forth with his hardy band of kinsmen and joining up with Jacobite sympathisers in southwest Scotland and northeast England, but they were captured at Preston.

Robert and Angus Shaw were taken south and imprisoned in the Tower of London.

Angus was among those Jacobites transported to Virginia, where he remained until he was pardoned in 1722. Returning to his Tordarroch estates he learned his brother, Robert, had died soon after his release from captivity in 1718.

Soured by his own experiences and the loss of his brother, Angus Shaw was understandably reluctant to lend his support to Prince Charles Edward Stuart's Rising of

1745, but numerous other Shaws rallied to the doomed cause.

By the time of the '45 Rising the chief of Clan Mackintosh was a captain in the Black Watch and had raised a company to fight on the government, or Hanoverian, side.

But this did not prevent his wife, the young and beautiful Lady Anne Mackintosh, from raising about 300 Chattan clansmen to fight for her prince.

Two of her main lieutenants in what became Lady Mackintosh's Regiment were a James and a John Shaw of Kinrara and, under the command of Colonel Alexander MacGillivray of Dunmaglas, the regiment fought with great distinction at the battle of Culloden on April 16, 1746.

Colonel MacGillivray was killed after the regiment, in the centre of the Jacobite front line, made a headlong charge into Barrel's Regiment.

Lady Anne, known as 'Colonel Anne', and whom the prince dubbed his 'belle rebelle', was imprisoned for a time at Inverness after this battle that dashed Jacobite hopes forever.

One of the most brutal of the Hanoverian commanders, Lieutenant-General Henry Hawley, known as 'Hangman Hawley', was so incensed with the deference with which his officers treated his beautiful and aristocratic captive that he infamously threatened: 'Damn the woman, I'll honour her with mahogany gallows and a silken cord!'

Fortunately for Lady Anne this proved to be an empty threat, and she was later released.

The colours of Lady Mackintosh's Regiment were the only ones not to be later ignominiously burned by the public hangman in Edinburgh. This was thanks to a Donald Mackintosh, who ripped them from the fallen and bloody standard, wrapped them around his body, and escaped from the carnage of the battlefield.

Chapter four:

Masonic heritage

Life for the Shaws of the Lowlands was no less exciting, but perhaps rather less marked with bloodshed than that of their Highland namesakes.

One of the earliest records of a Lowland Shaw relates to a John de Schawe who was a witness to a deed concerning Paisley Abbey, in the west of Scotland, in 1284, while Symon de Schawe, William de Schawe, and Fergus de Schawe, all from Lanark, were signatories to the infamous Ragman Roll of 1296.

Known as the Ragman Roll because of the profusion of ribbons that dangle from the seals of its signatories, the parchment was a humiliating treaty of fealty to England's Edward I, and the 1,500 bishops, earls, and burgesses such as the Shaws had little option but sign.

One Lowland Shaw, who not only stamped a personal mark on Scotland through his architecture but is also recognised as having laid the foundations of what has become Freemasonry, was William Schaw, of the Schaws of Sauchie, near Stirling.

The family had been appointed hereditary cupbearers, or keepers of the king's wine cellar, during the reign of Alexander III (1249-86), and this was reflected in armorial bearings that featured three covered cups.

James Schaw of Sauchie held the important position of governor of Stirling Castle in 1471, and was also entrusted as an ambassador to the English Court, while William Schaw, born in 1555, was at an early age a page to Mary of Guise, widow of James V and mother of the future Mary, Queen of Scots.

Later, as a skilled architect, James VI appointed him in 1583 as his Master of Works, overseeing the building, repair, and renovation of royal property in addition to carrying out lucrative private commissions.

William Schaw was also 'general wardene' of the stonemason craft in Scotland and in

December of 1598 issued the First Schaw Statute, aimed at regulating the craft in Scotland by laying down strictures against the employment of the semi-skilled and those not initiated into the craft.

He issued a second set of statutes a year later, and these hint at some of the more esoteric aspects of the craft that in later centuries became infused with what is now known as 'speculative', as opposed to 'craft' masonry, and better known as Freemasonry.

This is why William Schaw the architect, is recognised as one of the main 'architects' of a society that today can boast thousands of members throughout the world.

William Schaw acquired the barony of Sauchie in 1588, and on his death in 1602 Alexander Seton, Earl of Dunfermline, erected his magnificent tomb in Dunfermline Abbey. The Setons had been patrons of Schaw, and he had carried out work for them on Seton Palace.

Although born in Dublin in 1856, the great Irish playwright George Bernard Shaw is thought to have been of Scots descent through a Captain William Shaw who fought in Michelburn's Regiment for the cause of William III, better known as William of Orange, at the Battle of the Boyne in 1690.

Whatever his roots, George Bernard Shaw came to dominate the world stage as a dramatist, literary critic, defender of women's rights, and supporter of the cause of socialism.

Moving to London when he was aged 20, Shaw spent two years educating himself in the hallowed confines of the British Museum. His self-taught efforts paid off, resulting in plays such as *Major Barbara* and *Pygmalion*, later to become famous as the musical and film *My Fair Lady*.

He was awarded the Nobel Prize for Literature in 1925, but in keeping with his deeply held socialist beliefs, he refused the money. He died in 1950, aged 94.

One of the heroes of the battle of Waterloo in 1815 was a boxer known as Big Jack Shaw. Said to have been of prodigious strength, he served with the Life Guards, and is famed for having killed a number of Napoleon's elite French Cuirassiers in hand-to-hand combat.

In more contemporary times, Robert Shaw was the acclaimed writer and film actor whose films included *From Russia with Love*, *The Sting*, *A Man for all Seasons*, and *Jaws*. Born in Lancashire in 1927, he died in 1978.

Shaw is also the surname under which the American writer Irwin Shaw and jazz clarinettist Artie Shaw are better known. Born Irwin Gilbert Shamforoff in New York in 1913, Irwin Shaw, who died in 1984, was a prolific author of short stories, screenplays, and best-selling novels such as *The Young Lions* and *Rich Man, Poor Man*.

Born in New York in 1910, Arthur Jacob Arshawsky, was the pioneering composer, jazz clarinettist, and bandleader who, better known as Artie Shaw, contributed enormously to the whole jazz genre.

He was presented with a lifetime achievement Grammy Award in recognition of this significant contribution shortly before his death in 2004.